TAKE A WALK THROUGH MY MIND

BY ANGELA WIGNALL

Inspirational thoughts and poems to
help you cope with everyday life.

Published by New Generation Publishing in 2019

www.newgeneration-publishing.com

New Generation Publishing

For Betty and Ron

my Mum and Dad

*They never failed to be there for me,
with warmth, love and laughter.
In fact, they still keep in touch,
from the heavenly realms,
to comfort, encourage and support
our whole family.*

Contents

Take A Walk Through My Mind – The Poem........... 1

Maybe It Began At The Beginning 3

When Life Gets Mental 14

Now Lets Have A Laugh! 20

Me And The Universe 30

Feel The Love That Surrounds You 43

Gone In An Instant - So What Happens Next? 48

When Is The End Not The End? When It's The
Beginning! 52

Contents

Take A Walk Through My Mind

Take a walk through my mind.
There is plenty to find.
Life has shattered,
shaken and stirred me.

The rocks that abound,
I've fought hard to get around,
but, believe I have
conquered them bravely.

Read the poems in this book
and don't be afraid to look,
for a twinkle of recognition
in my words.

May your thoughts of me be kind,
as you walk right through my mind
and be sure to tell your friends
of the treasures that you find!

Composed by Angela

MAYBE IT BEGAN AT THE BEGINNING

When I was a little girl, at bedtimes and on family holidays at the seaside, mum and dad would read stories to my younger sister and I. As much as we loved hearing the adventures, mum and dad loved making each story and the characters within the books, come alive. I believe my enjoyment of the written word, began, during those happy days.

When a person reads a story, a poem, or a speech to an audience, there has to be expression in their voice and body language. Just like an actor on the stage, the performance needs to be entertaining.

Our dad had the ability to make the stories exciting and funny, so we were always laughing during his turn to tell the tale. He had a calming, gentle way of dealing with people and a charismatic telephone voice. At the age of fourteen, he successfully gained the position of Office Boy at Mathew Hall Engineering Company (where he continued his career for forty five years) because of his ability to use the telephone!

I remember when I was fifteen and just left school. I attended many interviews for secretarial vacancies, but was never offered a position. Then one day I was lucky to be interviewed by a lady, who often spoke on the telephone with dad, as a colleague, but had never met him. She asked me if he was tall, dark and handsome, as this was how she imagined him, when listening to his lovely voice. I didn't tell her that my dad was short, cuddly and bald and I got my first job! However, it was mum who introduced us to poetry. She had an amazing, deep and silky voice and a very expressive face, especially her eyes and eye brows!

Mum didn't have the opportunity to attend school regularly, because of the huge disruption to her life during the Second World War. She was born in 1929 and when she was about thirteen her mother and four of mum's younger siblings were evacuated to Yorkshire. Mum had secured an apprenticeship working in a milliner's shop, so she stayed behind in London and lived with her Aunty Gladys. The owners of the shop were very kind to mum and taught her how to make beautiful, stylish hats, realising that she had a natural talent for the work involved.

I remember mum telling us that one night during the war, she and her younger sister Mary had gone to bed in the family home, in the room they both shared. Later that night, my grandmother (who cared for the children on her own as granddad was a prisoner of war in Germany) decided to gather all of her children together and take them to the air raid shelter to sleep instead. In the morning when the family returned to the house, they discovered large shards of glass from the shattered windows, embedded in the pillows of the girls' bed. A bomb had exploded a short distance from their home.

It was whilst mum was working in the hat shop that she met dad one night, at a dance held in the Assembly Rooms, Wood Green, North London. Not long after their first encounter at the dance hall, dad decided to volunteer for the war and joined the Navy. Luckily for dad, after the war ended, he found mum waiting for him at the Assembly Rooms!

Mum carried the joy of creativity into her marriage with dad. She taught him how to knit and crochet and produce scrumptious cakes for birthdays and anniversaries. Mum and dad iced and decorated the cakes together and both the cakes and mum and dad, were greatly admired within the community!

The poem I vividly remember mum reciting to us is Full Moon by Walter de la Mare. I believe mum had learnt to recite this at school, as in those days, very often the children had to learn a poem off by heart and recite it to the rest of the class. At family parties as a child herself, mum would be asked to recite Full Moon to entertain aunties and uncles.

Several years after the Second World War ended, my sister and I also shared a bed. As our little faces peeped out from under the covers, mum would recite Full Moon in her husky, smoky, tones and wiggle her eye brows! We listened in a state of delicious fright! Full Moon is one of three poems in this book that I didn't compose myself, but I included it, as it means so much to me.

Full Moon

One night as Dick lay fast asleep,
Into his drowsy eyes
A great still light began to creep
From out the silent skies.

It was the lovely moon's,
For when he raised his dreamy head,
Her surge of silver filled the pane
And streamed across his bed.

So, for a while, each gazed at each.
Dick and the solemn moon.
Till climbing slowly on her way,
She vanished and was gone.

Composed by Walter de la Mare (1873 – 1956)

In 1960, when I was five years old, I began my school years at Noel Park School, which was situated at the top of Lymington Avenue, where we lived, in North London. My little sister would join me about eighteen months later. I was a very shy child and for the first few weeks of school, during breaks, I would stand with my back against the wall in the playground and not move. Indeed, I was such a fixture, that the birds used to poop on my woolly hat!

This stage of mum's life was overshadowed by thoughts of the "atom bomb" and the Four Minute

Warning received before it reached us and obliterated her world. She knew it was a five minute walk or a two minute run, to reach the school from our house. I never realised until I was blessed with children myself, the extent of her concern.

Although mum loved to read stories and poetry to us, I can't remember her actually writing poems herself, apart from once. My sister and I were about eight and ten and mum wrote a poem for each of us. The poems meant a lot to her because, when I was fifty years old, she wrote my poem out again, in the birthday card she gave me! This is what she wrote in 1965 and then again in 2005.

We have a little girl, her name is Angie.
She loves a roast beef dinner.
She has brown hair and dark brown eyes
and wants to get a little slimmer.
She doesn't like bed or crusty bread,
but oh for a lemon lolly.
And when day is done and she is tired,
she loves to cuddle her dolly.
Composed by my mum for me.

From the age of about seven, I would frequently inform mum, that I was beginning a new project. I would acquire a nice big writing pad and a fresh ball point pen and begin to write. I never, ever, finished a story, giving up after a couple of pages. I also enjoyed the thought of keeping a diary, but very often the only words on the snowy white pages were Forget What Did!

I realise now, why writing poetry gives me so much pleasure. I am able to complete a poem, from start to finish, in literally ten to twenty minutes!

When someone or something has stirred my emotions, I feel the urge to create. Then I think of the first line of the poem and the rest just flows. I cannot believe how quickly the poems take form. Most of the time, after I have finished writing, I read the poem and am amazed that it was me who actually produced it!

The first poem I ever wrote was for my mum. She loved dad giving her birthday and anniversary cards with lovely sentimental words inside. I remember dad forgot an anniversary one year and mum didn't speak to him for a week! My dad was actually a very openly loving person, who gave mum and us lots of cuddles. But, for some people, the words of love and praise inside these cards may be the only ones they receive, so it means a lot to them.

After reading and sending lots of cards over the years, I thought perhaps I could write something more personal myself, for someone close to me. Here is the very first poem I wrote in a birthday card for mum. I think I was in my late twenties at the time. My first poetic step!

A Poem For My Mum – Betty

No mum could ever mean as much
as my mum does to me.
I only need to lift the phone
and comfort comes to tea.

She always listens to my heart
then tells me what to do.
She's been my friend for many years.
I love her. Wouldn't you?

Composed by Angela about thirty five years ago

In those days, I was not "politically correct" when composing poetry, in fact, the phrase wasn't even invented then. Luckily our family shared a similar sense of humour, so I could get away with what I thought, were funny observations.

Mum and dad were both, short, plump and cuddly, as they liked to eat cream cakes, indeed, all cakes.

They enjoyed playing Pitch and Putt on the seafront at

Ramsgate, not far from where they owned a holiday caravan. Pitching and Putting was becoming harder to complete, because of their roundness. They were also baby-sitting for my sister, who had two small children, so they needed more energy. They decided to go on a diet and both lost two stone.

When dad retired he joined the Over 50's at the local leisure centre and took up swimming and badminton. Whereas, mum's weight loss provided her with the ability to beat the whole family at Pitch and Putt and Ten Pin Bowling!

We enjoyed wonderful family holidays at the caravan, situated between Broadstairs and Ramsgate on the Kent coast. There were many places to visit in the surrounding area and we were out and about, breathing in the fresh sea air, all day.

My sister and I found it slightly irritating that mum would always be looking for a loo. Of course, nowadays, finding the loo, at any event, is my top priority!

I have set the scene for the next poem, which I wrote in a card for mum and dad, to celebrate their 38th Wedding Anniversary. Luckily, it made them laugh.

Poem for Mum and Dad's 38th Wedding Anniversary

You two are a couple
who used to be fat,
but now you are thin,
there's no doubt of that!

You tried very hard
to get very trim,
now dad's an athlete,
keen to swim!

Mum enjoys babysitting.
(Is this true?)
She knits and she crochets
and goes to the loo!

Now, the end of this rhyme,
has come just in time,
or otherwise I'd get a wollop!

But let's just say this,
the couple are BLISS
and their cake making
improves with each dollop!

Composed by Angela (July 1989)

Because I enjoyed writing the poems for birthdays and anniversaries so much, I started to write them whenever I was inspired to do so. Friends and family would be really pleased to receive one written especially for them.

When mum died in 2006, my sister asked me to write a poem that I could read to the congregation at the funeral. I really tried hard to produce something worthy. On the day of the funeral, my mouth was so dry, I could hardly speak, as not only was it mum's funeral, I had never stood on a platform in front of so many people and read aloud one of my poems.

As mum died a few days before their fifty fifth wedding anniversary, the poem began with mum and dad's meeting at the Assembly Rooms and embraced their life together, including my sister and I, the grandchildren and even the caravan!

Remembering Betty

Everyone loves our mum and dad,
they're such a cuddly pair!
Anyone who visits them
will leave their troubles there!

They met when mum was just seventeen
and dad had drunk a tipple!
We can't remember any rows,
well maybe just a ripple.

From little kids, to grown up girls
with children of our own.
They've given us love and laughter,
always a happy home.

Mum was always there for us
when we came home from school.
She did our hair, and shortened skirts,
handmade dresses, she made cool.

When we got drunk, she had raw eggs,
ready to help our heads.
And if we spoke of big weddings,
she told us to elope instead!

She always called a greeting
as we walked in through the door.
And she always stood and waved goodbye,
until we couldn't see her anymore.

She loved her grandchildren,
a friend to them all
and couldn't wait to get down to the van.
The golf and the bowling, competitive stuff!
Everyone got beaten by nan!

This year mum and dad would have been married
for fifty five happy years.
We think that their great secret,
for a love that lasted so long,
was to hold hands and laugh with each other
and it seemed not much could go wrong.

So, although we've said goodbye to mum,
I'm sure she's in a great place.
That glorious tea shop in the sky,
with a great big smile on her face!

Composed by Angela – July 2006
(Mum loved a cup of tea!)

After mum died aged seventy eight, dad said he could probably do with a couple more years and then he would be ready to join her! In fact dad lived another eight years enjoying the comfort of their little warden assisted flat on the Ridgeway in Enfield. He also enjoyed the companionship of the neighbours, whom he and mum had befriended during the time they had spent there as a couple.

It was at this point in dad's life that our family suffered the tragic loss of our dearly loved daughter, Jessica, who died in a tragic accident during her final year at university.

I believe dad took Jessica's death much harder inside, than he showed to the family. He was being strong for my husband and I and Jessica's older brother. I am sure he was deeply shocked by the fact that his beautiful granddaughter had died, at the tender age of twenty two, leaving him, an old man, to carry on living. Six months after Jessica died, he called my sister at home to say he had fallen over and needed to go to hospital. I believe he had suffered a stroke, and when he left the hospital after a week or so, he had developed a form of dementia.

For the next few years, until his death at the age of eighty nine, my sister and I cared for dad on a daily basis.

He was able to live in the flat on his own and never attempted to wander off, thank goodness. He was still the same charming man everybody loved, but needed our help to continue living independently.

I actually look back on those days with fond memories, as I loved looking after him. I would arrive in the morning, about nine thirty and see all the clearing up to be done, but dad would say "Give us a cuddle and sit down and talk to me." I realised that having a hug and someone to talk to was more important to dad, than me doing the washing up. I also enjoyed something that I never thought I would, washing dad's feet, cutting his toenails and moisturising his old legs.

My sister asked me to write a poem for dad's funeral and I found the words came easily.

A Special Man

It's easy to describe a man
for his gentleness and charm.
With eyes that always sparkle
and a voice to soothe and calm.

It's easy to remember,
his cheeky smile and funny quips.
No unkind words were spoken
from those cream cake covered lips!

A man you could rely on
for a cuddle and good cheer.
Who would listen to your worries
whilst drinking delicious beer!

It was easy to accept his love
and give love in return.
Something so unconditional,
we didn't need to earn.

He is on this earth no longer
and for all it's very sad.
But, he is easy to remember
as this special man's
our dad.

Composed by Angela July 2014

I believe it was mum and dad's enthusiasm and obvious enjoyment of reading to my sister and I that eventually led to my love of writing poetry.

My sister Lesley has inherited the ability to create enchanting flower arrangements using dried flowers. She has an excellent eye for colour and uses this gift within her home and also with the clothes she wears. Lesley also makes amazing cakes and actually attended a cake decorating class with dad, when he first retired from Mathew Hall Engineering.

We are so grateful to our parents for their fantastic story-telling and creativity, which encouraged us to use our imagination.

WHEN LIFE GETS MENTAL

Although the family home was filled with warmth and laughter, there was also an ever present shadow, the shadow of depression.

Mum and dad suffered from periods of depression and were both plagued with, at times, crippling anxiety.

For many years they were given repeat prescriptions for anti-depressants and sleeping pills. Even when dad reached the grand old age of eighty nine, he was still asking the doctor to prescribe him a pill that would make him happy! Although dad had suffered with anxiety from a young age, he presented a socially competent exterior to the outside world. He was kind, gentle, intelligent and funny. He used to say he was like a little duck on a pond. On the surface he was swimming along calmly, but underneath the water, his little legs were paddling away in a panic.

Dad's anxiety didn't stop him from socialising, as he really loved people and had the ability to make everyone feel he was interested in them, which he was.

Mum was a lovely warm home-maker, with a wicked sense of humour! She was a good listener and when people talked to her, they felt they had known her for years. Unfortunately, her anxiousness prevented her from attending social occasions, except with close family. She never stopped dad from seeing his friends or joining clubs connected to his hobbies, but she preferred to stay at home.

Whilst writing this book I realise that mum's experience of the Second World War, as a young girl, would certainly have contributed greatly to her anxious state of mind.

Although my sister and I are very close, we think quite differently and it is I who inherited the anxiety gene from mum and dad.

My anxiety has never developed into depression

thankfully, but it has gradually increased in severity as I've grown older.

As a young woman, I couldn't understand why mum was consumed with apprehension weeks before a social event or trip to somewhere other than the caravan, but when the date actually arrived, she seemed to cope well and in our eyes, enjoyed herself.

I realise now from my own personal experience, that she lived her concerns and worries over and over in her mind, from the moment the event was mentioned, until she had to face it in real time. My anxiety vanishes completely when I am finally immersed in what I perceive as the dreaded event and I usually go on to enjoy the occasion, whatever it is, immensely. After my conquest of the current event, my brain immediately searches for the next one.

In the first poem I ever wrote about my anxiety, I describe these events like hurdles in a race. My husband looks forward to the party, dinner, holiday, as a positive event, whereas I see in front of me obstacles to be overcome and have to work hard to conquer my irrational fears – it's exhausting.

As a couple, we are quite busy socially and are luckily invited on holidays and different adventures with friends, as the over sixties like a challenge! So my hurdles build up before me and I sometimes struggle to cope. Clearly this is not a good way to live your life, for the health of your mind, body and spirit. As I had watched mum and dad consume so many pills during their life together and seen some of the side effects from taking those pills, I decided to avoid drugs altogether and try to control my fears with some Talking Therapy – talking to myself!

Here are some of the things I say to myself.

- My number one coping strategy is to say "Angela – Take deep breathes. Think of someone worse off than yourself. Now get on with it."

- When I am going to a social occasion I say "Angela – You don't have to be the life and soul of the party. Nobody will mind if you don't say a word. Just smile and try to relax."

- The most recent one is to say "Don't panic, don't panic – take one day at a time." I can't even manage to say Angela before that one!

Most of the worries in my life are very small, in fact minute, compared to many people. I know how lucky I am to have a roof over my head, plenty to eat and enough money to have a holiday. But, the anxiety is real and it can and does cause me mental and physical pain, which at times, can be severe.

I woke up in the middle of the night a few months ago, after having dreamt I was a runaway train, whizzing on down a track. I decided to try and write a poem that describes how I feel when my mind is filled with anxious thoughts, which I cannot seem to stop. The poem is called My Train Of Thought.

My Train Of Thought

My thoughts are like a runaway train,
whizzing on down the track.
Out of control, I can hear the wheels spin.
Clickety, clickety, clack.

Way in front of me, down the hillside,
I see a frightening drop,
that falls into a dark ravine
so I start to holler STOP!

I desperately need, to take control,
of this ever speeding train.
For if I don't, I'll go over the edge,
never to be seen again.

16

I'll put my feet upon the brakes
and press them very gently.
Concentrate on slowing down,
with all the strength that hides within me.

That's it, the wheels are calming down
and through the tunnel I see some light.
Live first one day, then the next
and with a little help, you'll be alright.

Now this train only journeys
one day at a time.
Taking rests at the station
for its own peace of mind.

Composed by Angela 2017

Thousands of years ago, when man and woman first walked the Earth, they lived in the present moment. Rising with the sun at dawn, they would travel miles hunting for food, collecting water to

drink and wood for the fire. When the sun disappeared at the end of the day, they talked and sang together around the fire, enjoying the much needed warmth, then lay down to sleep, gazed upon by a million twinkling stars, exhausted.

Now we are living in the twenty first century, the age of technology and most of us have food, water, shelter and warmth and generally plenty of leisure time to fill.

We can only see the stars in abundance from certain areas of the planet, because of too much artificial light. Information is blasted at us constantly, from T.V, radio, newspapers, mobile phones and social media. We are all feeling the overload, especially our children.

We have to consciously take time to think in the present. The modern word for this is mindfulness.

Each morning when I wake, I go downstairs quietly, make a cup of tea and take it back up to bed, where I meditate for ten minutes, before the rest of the house stirs. Holding the warm cup in my hands, I say a thank you to the universe for all my blessings. Then I mentally send thoughts of love to any friends and family who may need healing and even to our planet Earth.

My great escape from the hustle and bustle of modern life is the Peak District, in Derbyshire. From when our two children were little and now just my husband and I, we have rented a small cottage in a tiny village there for one week. All around us are mountains, streams and sheep!

The minute I jump in the car for the journey up to the cottage, my mind is in the present moment. I don't think of future holidays, social occasions, problems at home, the problems of the world. I live in a bubble for a week and then when I begin the journey home, all the thoughts I have blanked out hit me like an avalanche.

People may think, what on earth have you got to complain about? You have a comfortable life and have no reason to be anxious compared with many people in this world. I have heard this said to people suffering with depression and who seem to have everything they need to be happy and content, yet are in despair.

Mental illness cannot be seen, measured and in some cases, understood. I am very lucky to be a level headed person, who can manage their anxiety issues, with Talking Therapy and a pen!

In 1987, after the sorrow of three miscarriages, my husband and I were blessed to have our son, Alex. Nineteen months later our beautiful daughter, Jessica was born and we were a family of four.

Our son suffered with anxiety from an early age (he is very much like his granddad Ron) and found the school environment extremely difficult to deal with. When Alex reached the age of twenty-one, he was diagnosed with Crohns (a chronic inflammatory bowel disease). I am sure that coping with the symptoms of Crohns as a child magnified his anxiety a hundred fold. Thankfully now he is a confident and caring individual who enjoys his life to the full.

The diagnosis of Crohns Disease in young people has grown by more than 300% over the last few years. No one actually knows whether stress and anxiety cause the development of Crohns Disease, but the pressures of our modern day society definitely inflame the inflammation! A few years ago, when I arrived home after leaving the Peak District, I wrote this poem.

Tumbling Through My Life

Rolling, tumbling, stumbling
through my life.
Push my heels in, try to slow down,
feel I'm slipping on ice.

I need to stop, just for a moment
and allow my mind to ease.
Hear the birds sing, feel the sun shine,
the cool of a breeze.

Listen to the waves
as they break on the shore.
Feel warm sand between my toes.
Beautiful sea shells galore.

Walk the earth with bare feet
my eyes seeking the stars.
A quiet promise of peace
fills the still night hours.

Composed by Angela – May 2014

NOW LETS HAVE A LAUGH!

Laughter is amazingly beneficial to our wellbeing and produces endorphins, which dance through our body, making us feel happy. If we laugh every day, especially with family and friends, we make positive energy, which is good for our overall health.

You may not have the comfort and support of family and friends to laugh with, so try enjoying a funny film or read a book that encourages you to smile.

If you are suffering with depression, thoughts of laughing must seem utterly impossible and not even desirable. Smiling, even if you feel awful, can make life seem a tiny bit better. It's a start.

In this section of the book, I have included poems which, hopefully, will bring a smile to your face. A friend remarked once how she enjoyed my work, (those were her words and I was thrilled), as my poems always end on a positive note, which is uplifting. I do try to always look for the silver lining. I can find it, most of the time.

The first poem, which may produce a smile is called Beware Of The Duck! When we visit the Peak District, we have a favourite circular bicycle ride through a valley surrounded by green and craggy hills. We usually stop half way around, at a picturesque beauty spot, to have a picnic lunch. A small stone bridge straddles a bubbling stream. Large boulders are scattered amongst the trees and a fallen log provides a seat where we can munch on our sandwiches. Perfect!

As this is a favourite spot for many walkers and cyclists to stop, over the years several ducks have decided to have their lunch there too. On this particular day, my husband and I stopped by the log and parked our bikes. There were no other people about and certainly no sign of ducks.

We unpacked our sandwiches, packets of crisps and a flask of tea and settled down. A whooshing sound over by the stream attracted our attention to a group of ducks, landing on the water. Waddling in our direction from the cover of the trees, more ducks. Then the duck from hell appeared from behind a boulder, just in front of us.

She quickly goes for my ankles, snapping and quacking! We are surrounded now by hungry ducks, only this particular duck, brave enough, or mad enough, to attack. "Clear off!" shouts my husband, as he kicks out with his boot. Over goes the flask and the tea disappears into the grass. "Don't kick the duck!" I screech as the duck proceeds to nip at my legs. "I'm not kicking the duck, I'm indicating it should CLEAR OFF!" As bread and cheese from his sandwich scatter at our feet, the she monster is driven mad for more!

"That's it!" I cry, "I'm clearing off!" I packed up my uneaten sandwich, flask and what was left of my crisps, jumped on my bike, leaving the husband in the company of ducks and escaped into the woods. We had met that particular duck, in the exact same spot, on a previous occasion, but thought she might not have spotted us this time. When we looked back at the duck attack, we had a good laugh, but will choose a duck free spot on future rides.

Beware Of The Duck!

Pedalling down the hillside,
looking forward to my lunch.
A horrid thought occurred to me
and it wasn't just a hunch.

There's a little bridge across a stream,
where I stop to enjoy the view.
Of course I bring my sandwiches
and this is nothing new.

But, there is a duck, who awaits me there
and she'll try hard to eat my dinner.
Nipping at my calves and toes,
I'd really like to skin her!

21

She won't give up and quacks and struts.
A duck sent straight from hell!
I think she knows she's frightening me
and she's doing it really well!

I scramble up to pack my stuff
and jump back on my bike.
If you want to keep your picnic,
this is not the place to hike.

Composed by Angela - Peak District 2016

I have always enjoyed being outdoors and when my sister and I were young children and living on a council estate, although the garden was very small, I loved to be there, making mud pies! I had a red bicycle which I named Rudolf and I would cycle around our block of terraced houses again and again, but I would never go off the pavement, always staying close to home. Dad took us to the park at weekends to fish for tadpoles in the ponds and I loved being out in the open so I could see the sky and play amongst the lovely trees of the wooded areas.

My husband and I discovered we both loved walking in nature early on in our relationship. Sunday afternoons we spent strolling through Victoria Park in the East End of London. After a few years we discovered the lakesides of Buttermere in the Lake District and eventually the hills and mountains of the Peaks. So it was not surprising that when we married, we chose to live within walking distance of the forest.

Our present home is in a quiet tree lined road just a short walk from the forest. I have made very good friends with my neighbours and talked often about our holidays in the Peak District and our bicycle rides through the forest. They suggested we all walk together one day and that's when our band of neighbourly walkers began their forest walks.

Three or four ladies would meet me every couple of

weeks outside my house at 10.30 am. We would amble about in the forest, walking five to six miles and stop for a cheese roll, cup of tea and piece of cake at the green hut in High Beech, Essex. My husband said we were a female version of Last Of The Summer Wine! These walks continued for over twenty years and provide very fond memories.

The Neighbourly Walkers

"Are you OK for Thursday, 10.30 dressed for rain?"
Its time for the neighbourly walkers
to be organised again.

I rush around then leave the house, walking stick in hand
and wait upon the pavement, for my neighbourly
rambling band!

One by one we gather, all different shapes and sizes!
"Shall I wear a scarf today,
or perhaps I need sunglasses?"

Once we all get started, we're off on our forest walk.
It's very therapeutic,
as we share a lot of talk.

We try to halt our chatter and stop to hug a tree.
Or quietly look at nature,
wildlife we hope to see.

We reach our destination, a hut so green and welcoming.
Thoughts of cheese rolls and pieces of cake
have kept our mouths a watering!

As we sip our tea,
we all agree.
This is the very best place that we could be!

Composed by Angela – September 2011

I never returned to a secretarial career after I became a mum, preferring a series of part-time jobs, working with children of all ages, my favourite being Fidgety Fingers Pre-School Nursery.

A very good friend of mine knew that I only wanted to work one morning a week. At that time I was going twice a week into my children's school to help out voluntarily, invigilating at a secondary school and helping my mum and dad with a bit of cleaning and shopping. I really wanted to work on a Tuesday morning, so when she phoned to say she was starting a new Pre School and would I like to work with her one morning a week, a Tuesday, I couldn't believe my luck!

I enjoyed every minute of working at Fidgety Fingers from when I entered the nursery at 9.00am to when I left at 1pm. It was a small, cosy, extremely well run environment, with only about twelve children on a daily basis. The children had to refer to us as Aunty and it made for a closer bond to each child.

As you approached the nursery from the small driveway, there were wind chimes, pots full of pretty flowers and little gnomes with smiley faces, all intended to welcome you. It was like walking into fairyland! At the back of the nursery there was a large garden with a slide and sand pit. When the children had their snacks, if the weather permitted, they would sit on a rug under a beautiful tree and I would be privileged to read them a story. My friend told me the children sat mesmerised by my ability to make the story come alive. (All thanks to mum and dad!)

I loved seeing the little children progress from their first tentative days to when they left to start big school. I wrote the following poem from the eyes of a child, imagining how they would feel attending this lovely haven each day.

Fidgety Fingers – My Nursery

I open my eyes and its sunny, the birds are chirping away.
From somewhere downstairs I hear mum call
"Wake up sleepy, its nursery today!"

I jump out of bed in my PJs, excited to get to the door.
I'm going to Fidgety Fingers,
I won't lie in bed anymore.

I love to go to my nursery, to see all my friends and have
fun.
To play on the slide in the garden,
jump in the sand and to run!
When we're tired we'll sit in the sunshine,
having a drink and a snack.
The Aunties will read us a story, they always keep us on
track!

Perhaps we might do some painting,
or make salt dough models inside.
Draw a beautiful picture, to take home to mummy with
pride.

Dad says that Fidgety Fingers encourages the best out of
me.
I just can't wait to get there
and stay all day long till my tea!

Composed by Angela – May 2013

As I approached the age of fifty, I started to notice
more the pressure put upon us in the media to look young,
especially women. For years, while all my friends were
dying their hair, I let the gentle scattering of salt and
pepper grey appear in my own hair, much to their disdain!
It was only when, seated next to my sister-in-law's mother,
who was in her eighties at the time, I realised we had the

same style and colour hair, I thought perhaps I should address the issue!

There followed ten years of colouring my hair myself at home (as I begrudge spending a fortune in the hair dressers)! I started off with varying shades of brown, which was quite successful. I remember feeling amazing when the first person said "You look ten years younger." Achievement!

After a few years of colouring, I began to get fed up with putting chemicals on my head. Because I was trying to use the hair dye a little less frequently, my colour had gradually evolved into a unique blend of orangey, silvery, grey. People seemed impressed with this look and would actually enquire which hairdresser I used!

It was around this time two things happened. One, I suddenly thought, why do we ladies have to keep covering our grey hair and two, grey became the new blonde!! I stopped colouring my hair altogether and awaited the breath taking attention I would receive, when my hair was finally a natural shade of grey! Didn't happen!

The first poem I wrote to explain my feelings on the issue of looking younger is called The Mature Lady. A couple of years later I produced, The Mature Lady Rebels!

The Mature Lady

Wow!
It's great to be sixty.
What an honour I'm still alive on this day.
I feel I'm allowed to be grown up,
so I'm letting my hair go all grey.

Some people will scream
'No don't do it!"
'It's not time to let yourself go!"
But, I feel that I want to be natural,
the wisdom of old age to show.

Why is it wrong
to have wrinkles and silver hair?
It shows we've been here a long time.
On the way we've experienced hard times,
and can now teach our young ones to shine.

So I'm letting you see that I'm sixty
and I'll smile with a warmth and a glow.
Just ask my advice if you need it.
For surely at my age I'll know.

Composed by Angela – October 2015

The Mature Lady Rebels!

I am finally a real Mature Lady,
with silver hair surrounding my head!
But now I've achieved this great status,
I want to be a red head instead!

There are so many grey foxes abounding
for its cool and its trendy and fab!
But now I feel I want to see colour,
even if it does come out of a lab!

Though, whatever the colour my hair is,
be sure to remember one fact.
In my heart lives a passionate woman
I think you can be sure of that!

Composed by Angela – January 2018

I wanted to see what my hair looked like naturally grey
and I achieved that. Because grey hair has (at the time of
writing) become fashionable, millions of women feel they
don't have to rush for the dye immediately a grey hair
appears. Now they can decide whether to colour their hair
if they wish and have an abundance of colours to choose

from. I have chosen to experiment with colour for a little while longer!

The last poem in this section is called A Light Hearted Look At Religion. When I was a little girl my favourite subject in my primary school was Religious Instruction, as it was called then. I loved sitting at the desk, quietly listening to the teacher Mr. Grimm, tell us about the stories of the bible.

I remember the first time I ever thought about dying. I was around eight years old, sitting on the sofa watching the television (in black and white) with mum and my sister. I thought "When I die, I'll never see Coronation Street again, ever!" I imagined everything would just go black. Since then, I have had an insatiable appetite to learn about anything to do with the universe and what happens to us when we die.

Although we didn't attend church as a family, mum would read my sister and I stories about Jesus. I loved Jesus and always said my prayers before I went to bed, knowing he would look after me. Later on in life, whilst discussing romantic loves with friends, I said I had only ever loved Jesus, Cliff Richard and my husband!

I was lucky that my dad shared a similar passion for seeking answers to questions about the universe, God and different religions. We used to visit the library together on Saturday afternoons. When I married and moved out of the family home, dad and I would lend each other books we found interesting on these subjects and discuss them when I popped in for a cuppa.

I hope the following poem doesn't offend anybody, but can be taken in the light hearted way it was intended.

A Light Hearted Look At Religion

What religion are you?
The form states quite boldly.
I suppose I am a Christian,
I'll put down C of E.

Now hold on a minute,
let me give this some thought.
Am I really C of E
or is that just what I've been taught.

There are some that try Kabbalah
and others Scientology!
These are weird and wonderful,
but I don't think they're for me.

My Aunty is a Catholic
which can be complicated.
A Humanist is popular,
but I think is overrated.

Perhaps I should be a Buddhist.
Sit crossed legged and chant all day.
Or maybe practice Yoga.
That might help me find
THE WAY

I think I know the answer.
All these religious paths,
should lead to the same conclusion
God is love within our hearts.

So when I'm asked to tick a box
that defines my religion,
the one marked OTHER
should be right.
There, I've made my decision.

Composed by Angela – July 2011

ME AND THE UNIVERSE

As I entered my teenage years, I attended a particularly rough school and Jesus abandoned me for a while.

I didn't pass my eleven plus exam, so at first was placed in a Secondary Modern school called Parkwood School for Girls. I flourished in an ordered environment, where we were encouraged to learn. I particularly enjoyed school assembly in the mornings, where I sung so happily at the top of my voice, as if my lungs would burst! I still have the very hymn book I was given by the Head Mistress.

After one year at Parkwood, comprehensive schooling was introduced to the Educational System. All the girls in my school were redistributed to different schools in the area, where we had to integrate with boys. I was placed in the new Wood Green Comprehensive School, where most of the pupils didn't want to learn, but did want to FIGHT, FIGHT, FIGHT!

The only lesson I enjoyed during these few years was English and that was because of the teacher, Miss Grey. She managed the unruly class with her ready wit and fascinating explanations. We would listen to, discuss and debate, poetry and literature. And yes, Miss Grey did have grey hair! She was young, very pretty and always wore short skirts. No wonder those bad boys behaved themselves during her class.

When I wanted to leave school at the age of fifteen, Miss Grey (together with dad) convinced me to stay on and sit my exams. I eventually left in the summer of 1971 with a Grade I CSE, which was equivalent to an O Level and a Shorthand Typing certificate.

These two qualifications were actually very useful for my intended career as a secretary.

I worked in the heart of London for three different companies, over a period of five years. I thoroughly enjoyed being a secretary with varied challenges, meeting new people and like dad, I was told I had a good telephone voice.

Although I was enjoying my life in London, I knew I wanted to leave the family home and be independent, but I couldn't afford it. We lived in a council house and mum and dad had no money to lend me. I wasn't clever enough to gain a university degree, so the student lifestyle wasn't an option. I decided to be an Au Pair and live abroad!

Through a company I had worked for, Anglo European Liaison, I acquired a position with a family in Rome. Mum was devastated by the news. She had never been abroad herself and not only was she anxious beyond words about her twenty year old daughter, going to live in a country she had never been to before, to live with a family she had never met, mum would miss my rent money. As the time for my departure drew near, I bought mum a plant from Woolworths to make her feel better.

It was during my four month stay in Italy that I met my first Earth Angel!

I believe angels do exist, but it has taken me years to understand what they are and where they come from. From reading books and talking with friends, I know they have different roles to play and have beautiful names like Raphael, Gabriel and Zadkiel. Probably the most well known angel is Archangel Michael.

In recent years, I have heard of angels who are actually in human form. Many of my friends are so kind and supportive I often call them Earth Angels! But, I will always remember an incident in Rome, during my time as an Au Pair, when I believe I was rescued by a real Earth Angel!

When the plane landed late at night in Rome airport, I was met by a distinguished middle aged man holding a large card with my name on it. This was my host for the next four months. He whisked me off in a black limousine, to an apartment a few streets away from St. Peter's Basillica.

It was only when the sun shone through a crack in the

31

blinds that first morning and I heard the laughter of a four year old child, that I fully realised what I had done. I had no experience of looking after young children whatsoever at that time in my life! I needn't have worried, I only had one child to look after, a little boy called Nikki and we got on famously.

I met my Italian Earth Angel about three weeks into my stay. It was my day off and I had been sightseeing all over the city. I wasn't keeping an eye on the time and I realised I was going to be late home. The gentleman I was working for was a Member of Parliament and he and his wife were going out to attend a special dinner.

Suddenly, a storm was overhead and torrential rain pummelled the streets, leaving rivers of rain gushing over the pavements and I was soaked to the skin. I was running frantically down the street in the direction of the apartment, when a car pulled in at the side of the road just in front of me.

I don't know why, but I stopped and looked in the window of the car and saw a priest beckoning me to open the door and get in. I did! He didn't utter a word and neither did I (I couldn't catch my breath through running). I felt completely safe. He drove about ten minutes through the now deserted streets, to the apartment. I turned and said thank you in Italian and he smiled. I'd arrived, drenched, just in time. I suppose you could think that being so near St. Peters, there would be many priests driving about. But I will always remember the incident as magical!

The time I spent in Italy as an Au Pair was good for me. It gave me confidence in the knowledge I could look after myself. Not only did I navigate the perils of living in a foreign city, I also spent a few weeks in the country home of Nikki's grandparents.

The family and I drove to their large mansion situated in a remote mountain village. To my horror, Nikki's parents departed immediately for a summer holiday by the sea and we were left to make the most of our stay in the company of the aged Grandmother, (who was extremely eccentric and very scary) Grandpa, and a one eyed cook called Alba, none of whom could speak English.

By the time I was due to travel home, looking forward to a roast beef dinner and seeing my family, I could speak pretty good conversational Italian. I only have happy memories of that time and the people I met during my stay.

Over the years I've learnt more about angels and how they are able to help us during our life time, here on planet Earth. I have been told that the word angel means "messenger". They are meant to bring love and harmony into our lives and help us stay calm, eventually bringing peace to our world.

A good friend of mine, Penny, loved angels, especially Archangel Michael. When we met for lunch or coffee and a cake, she would attempt to answer my many questions about these Divine beings.

I met Penny when I took my own children to school. She and I would be the first mums through the school gates in the mornings and that's where our friendship began. Sadly my dear friend passed to the angels herself from a cancer related illness and never got to hear the poem I wrote for her called A Prayer To The Angels.

A Prayer To The Angels

When it seems the world is going mad
hold on.
When you wake up feeling really sad
hold on.

Amongst the dark and gloomy,
I see a glow of light.
Many angels with their mighty swords,
it's such a glorious sight!

Shimmering wings of power
to keep us safe from harm.
Whispering words of comfort
to help us all stay calm.

They've come to heal the planet
and fill our world with love.
I prayed "Dear God will you help us now."
And they came from up above.

Composed by Angela

When I returned home from Italy in September 1976, I was lucky to find another secretarial position very quickly. Mum was especially pleased because I could start giving her some much needed cash again!

I had decided to look for a job locally, as for the past few years, working in the centre of London, I had spent a considerable amount of time caught up in the many bomb scares, associated with the IRA.

Frequently, tube stations were quickly closed down. I would have to find a way home amongst the chaotic, frightened commuters, by bus and at times, on foot. So when I was offered the post of Senior Secretary in a large engineering company called Cryoplants (a subsidiary of BOC) I was very relieved.

The office buildings and large factory were situated on the North Circular Road near Edmonton, North London, not far from the North Middlesex hospital where I was born. I travelled to work by bus initially and later, when I could afford it, my own little car.

Although I worked hard during the eleven years I spent at Cryoplants, I also had a lot of fun. These were the days of a two hour lunch break and when we weren't visiting the pub, I enjoyed jogging along the canal footpath (the River Lea)) a chess club and even a swim in the nearest pool, which was Edmonton. I thoroughly enjoyed my time working at Cryoplants and still see many of the friends I made there.

I have always been interested in people and friendships are very important to me. I do make an effort to keep in touch with friends and most of them are pleased that I do!

All my friendships have individual aspects of specialness. My friends have each added to the mix of what makes me the person I am today and I am really pleased to say that my husband is one of my closest friends. We met in the early seventies when I was fifteen and he was seventeen and a week away from passing his first driving test. I sometimes wonder what would have happened if he had failed, as he lived two long bus journeys away from me!

Some of my oldest friendships were made in my secondary school days, in that noisy classroom, full of unruly boys and girls. One very dear friend who came from a Grammar School was placed next to me for Maths. She very kindly let me copy her work when I was falling behind and we always achieved 10/10! Another school friend often pops up in my dreams to save me, like a super hero. I have told her she must be a mighty space warrior during her sleep state!

Other friendships grew during my own children's school days. I volunteered to work in their nursery and primary school, helping with cookery, artwork, listening to readers, day trips and the school fete. Through these activities I made a very close group of friends which included Penny. I still meet up every couple of weeks for lunch with these lovely ladies.

My husband and I have many shared friends, who we have known for years and socialise with them together. As with a marriage, you have to spend some time to nurture these relationships, but I feel blessed to have so many friends who care about our wellbeing.

We were never in more need of our own close relationship and the support of our friends and family, than when our precious daughter, Jessica, died the day before her twenty-second birthday.

No one knows how they will cope with such a loss and people find it almost impossible to think of the 'right' words to say to the bereaved. In reality, there are no 'right' words to embrace everyone, as everyone gains comfort differently. I was extremely fortunate that my friends managed to be there for me and support me in a way that was right for me.

I needed that initial hug with no spoken words. To carry on normally, until I felt able to talk about Jessica, how she died and how thoroughly she had lived. And they would listen and smile and wipe away my tears.

I was having tea and cake with my Grammar School friend recently and the thought came to me, you are my sister of the universe!

I wrote the following poem and sent it to her and then realised I wanted all my friends to know how much I appreciate them, so they all got one!

Sisters Of The Universe

We're sisters of the universe.
I know you oh so well.
You listen with your heart
and mind,
whilst my truths
to you I tell.

Your friendship is
so precious
and has helped me on
my way.
Given me strength and courage
to embrace each and every day.

I believe our paths
were meant to cross
and hope we will remain,
travellers in time and space,
sharing lifetimes again and again!

A poem for my lovely friends.
With Thanks

Composed by Angela 2017

I have read very different views on reincarnation. Buddhist's believe that we begin the next life as soon as we finish this one. They believe we may even reincarnate as an ant or a fly for instance and treat every life form, here on Earth, as though it may be their beloved relative in their new existence.

Other books tell us that we don't have to live another life here on Earth at all if we don't wish to. Planet Earth is our school of learning. We are tossed about here and given opportunities to choose between good or bad deeds. Ultimately, we are here to learn that good is best, in order to progress to higher levels in our continued existence out there, somewhere in our majestic universe.

I believe the universe, everything we can see and even what we cannot see, is made up of tiny particles of energy, vibrating at different speeds and that includes us. When the physical body dies, our soul or the energy essence of us, moves into another dimension and lives on. It is exciting to learn that groups of young physicists from all over the globe are coming to an astonishing conclusion: the world we experience is continually branching into parallel universes.

I wrote the next poem whilst on holiday in the Peak District, an area we have been visiting for over twenty-five years and where I feel so comfortable. I actually believe I may have lived a past life there, perhaps as a maid or inn-keeper's wife, or even a shepherdess!

Most of my holidays as a child were spent either in Walton-on-the-Naze or Jaywick Sands, near Clacton-on-Sea, Essex. In those days, these were pretty little seaside towns, with clean yellow sands, donkey rides and plenty of ice cream!

We only had one holiday a year and would travel to Clacton by train with extended family, including aunts, uncles, cousins and my mum's parents. We all fitted into one carriage and had a picnic on the train, whilst singing songs from the forties and fifties, all the way to the seaside. The little children and the old nanny and granddad would eventually fall asleep to the sound of the train's wheels on the tracks, clickety clack, clickety clack, clickety clack.

My days of spending holidays with mum and dad at the seaside ended at the age of sixteen, when I was invited by a friend to join her and her parents on my first holiday abroad, to Spain. Mum said "Why do you want to go abroad, it will be just like Clacton." But I wanted to see for myself!

In the late seventies, before we were married, my husband to be encouraged me to join him on a back packing trip to Greece, which was another nightmare for mum! We bought one back pack and borrowed another, as we didn't have much money at the time and were gone for three weeks. No mobile phones in those days, in fact I don't think we had a telephone at home at the time.

We stayed in Athens for two nights and then travelled by ferry to a group of Greek Islands called the Cyclades. When we arrived in the tiny fishing harbour of Paros, we were surrounded by many Greek gentlemen offering us a place to stay in their family homes.

We followed the least dubious of these characters, along narrow cobbled streets, to his home where we spent several nights sleeping in the front parlour, sharing the bathroom facilities with his large family! This unusual form of accommodation was generally the norm on our three week adventure around these islands. After we were married and had a little more money, we were able to hire a scooter when we visited Greece again and stay in small hotels.

On Corfu and Rhodes, we sped along the sunny sand swept lanes, on the edge of the sea, with the wind in our hair!

When we were a family of four and our two children were little, we loved spending time on the Spanish island, Menorca. Another island, the Isle of Wight, situated off the south coast of England, was a magical place where we have many happy memories of our times together. Thankfully, there was no scary, hairy old man to greet us when we arrived on the ferry!

For many years we enjoyed the company of our son and daughter on our family holidays together, even to the Peak District, but as they grew into their teenage years, they decided they wanted to have a different kind of fun and began to holiday with their friends.

On the day I wrote the next poem, my husband and I had enjoyed a long walk amongst the bluebells, through a wood, beside a stream, whilst spending a few days in the Peak District. I was enchanted with the peace and natural beauty and I thought I must write a poem to help me remember the day.

I have been very lucky to have received so much love during my life, but I do try hard to see the good in people. If someone does or says something unkind to me or to my family or friends, I always look at why that person could have behaved in that way. Perhaps they were having a really awful day, or something in their life was making them unhappy at the time.

I avoid confrontation, but am not afraid to give my opinion on something, as long as it doesn't hurt anybody. After spending sixty three years on this planet, I have found that people respond positively, when spoken to with kindness. Confrontational or aggressive behaviour inflames the situation, although I do enjoy a bit of heated debate with the husband!

The Bluebell Wood

Did I just see a fairy,
as I walked down by the stream?
I felt so at one with nature,
but it may have been a dream.

Her fairy wings were sparkling
as the bluebells called her name.
She seemed to smile and flew on by
enjoying her fairy game.

I had to watch my footsteps
as I walked along the path.
For the wise old trees had spread their roots,
and it was difficult to pass.

Soon I came upon a bridge,
where the tinkling water flowed
and I saw the fairy settle
on a grumpy, lumpy toad!

I was blessed to see the fairy,
as she lifted her tiny wand
and sprinkled star dust on the toad,
so that all his troubles were gone!

I lay down on the soft green moss
and closed my eyes to rest.
The fairy whispered in my ear.
Choose to love, it's always best.

Composed by Angela – In the Peak District

Of all the poems I have written over the years, The Bluebell Wood is one of my favourites. It takes my breath away when I read it, imagining the beautiful little fairy carrying her tiny wand and everyone knows a grumpy lumpy toad!

I believe that I am helped and inspired in my writing by the angels and my loved ones who have gone on before me into the next dimension. One day, whilst preparing the evening meal in the kitchen, I heard John Lennon singing the song "Imagine" on the radio. I suddenly had the thought to write a poem for the world, to remind them of the significance of the words! What am I like!

As Planet Earth is our school of learning, I can understand that we need to experience life here with all its traumas, happiness, pain and sorrows for the progression of the soul, but as I have grown spiritually, I feel the pain of fellow human beings and animals, indeed any living thing that suffers, anywhere in the world, as I know we are all connected.

Being highly sensitive and feeling everybody's pain is not actually good for your own general health and wellbeing. You have to try and find a balance of giving love and compassion to those close to you and to your community, but especially to yourself, or your energy starts to deplete. You can't heal everyone, everywhere, but your loving intentions will ripple out across the planet and help the world to be a better place for us all.

Here is the poem I wrote after listening to "Imagine" sung by John Lennon.

Peace on Earth – Our Future

John Lennon sang "Imagine"
and I believe the time is near,
when man will love his fellow man
and all religions disappear.

The truth, that we are all the same,
made of cosmic energy.
One day will be a knowledge
received with joy and clear for all to see.

Until that day we have to strive
to care for one another.
Look at every living being
as if they are your brother.

We must not forget the plants and animals,
who share our precious planet.
Responsibility rests with human beings,
for the special things that live upon it.

So, be strong, be wise.
Don't just think of now.
The next generation are our future.
May their thoughts of us be wow!

Composed by Angela for the World

FEEL THE LOVE THAT SURROUNDS YOU

Jessica and her brother Alex were so close when they were little and clearly loved each other very much. I have so many photographs of the two of them laughing, arms around each other's shoulders, facing the world together. Jessica wasn't an anxious child, quite the opposite and really enjoyed going to school, looking forward to making new friends and facing life's challenges.

When Jessica died suddenly, the shock to the whole family was immense. Because I was blessed to have the knowledge that she had gone on into the next stage of her life in another dimension, I was able to help comfort our family and Jessica's friends.

Our deceased loved ones can produce physical signs to let us know they are still close to us. I have no idea how they do it, but I will share a few amazing examples of this.

On the night we learned of Jessica's death, of course we couldn't sleep. I came downstairs in the middle of the night to make a cup of tea and as I walked into the kitchen the first thing I saw was a newspaper, folded in half and left on a chair. Just one word filled the page, MUM.

The next morning I was desperately trying to find the passage in a spiritual book I had read, thirty years ago, that describes the dimension I knew Jessica had passed to. My husband had listened patiently over the years, whilst I talked about the afterlife, but I felt he needed to see it written down in black and white, at this crucial moment in our life together, to try and bring him some comfort and hope.

As I found the pages I needed, I was so excited I did something I have never done before or since. I ran forward and sort of jumped onto a small step in front of our French windows leading onto the garden. I yelled 'Yes!' and as I did that, I must have let out a breath onto the window pane, because as I looked, a smiley face appeared in the

43

moisture in front of me, then slowly disappeared. I shouted "It's a miracle!"

About a week before Jessica's funeral, I decided to buy a red jacket to go over the black dress I was going to wear. I drove to a large outdoor shopping area and parked the car. I found a red jacket straight away, but was not sure of the size I would need, so was in the changing room for a long time saying to Jess "Shall it be this one or that one?" I finally made the choice, paid and walked back out into the sunshine.

As I walked towards my dark blue car, I could see something red underneath. It was a balloon, the same colour red as my new jacket, lodged just under the front of the car! I looked all around the car park, but could see no other balloons in sight. I bent down and pulled the balloon free and the words Mr. Happy were written on it. I took this as a sign Jessica was happy with my choice!

I wanted to look my best at the funeral so Jessica would be proud of me, so I decided I should have my hair done at the hairdressers Jessica used, just before she passed. She had told me how much she enjoyed the young girl's conversation as she did her hair and that she would definitely go back there next time.

I made an appointment with the same young lady, but decided not to tell her about Jessica's passing, as it would be upsetting for her. She talked to me about how I would like my hair to look and then directed me to the sink to have my hair washed.

As I lay my head back and the water started to cover my hair, I closed my eyes. I could SEE Jessica. Not in my mind's eye, but right there between my eyes and my eye lids. I saw her head and shoulders and there was a rose coloured haze all around her. She moved slightly and didn't actually smile widely, but looked serene.

I opened my eyes, no Jessica, only the hustle and bustle of the hairdressers getting on with their jobs. I closed my eyes again and there she was. I thought "Jessica has come to let us know she survives and is well!" Then I had to open my eyes because they had finished washing my hair and she was gone. That experience has never happened again in the eight year's since Jessica passed, but it gave me the strength to cope with her funeral and I will never forget that gift.

The last example of how our deceased loved ones can cross that bridge of love between two worlds to help us, concerns my mum and dad.

When my sister was twelve years old, she had to be rushed to the Elizabeth Garret Anderson hospital in London and was admitted to a gynaecological ward for adults, as she was suffering with a women's problem.

She had to stay in the hospital for about two weeks and as mum was of a nervous disposition and couldn't bring herself to go up on the train, dad visited in his lunch break from work. I was at school at the time, but went to visit at the weekends with dad. My mum had packed my sister's hospital bag and because she couldn't be there herself she had included two white teddy bears. My sister and I were given a teddy each, by our paternal grandmother, when we were babies.

Forty-eight years later and a few months after dad died, my sister was due to have another procedure in the Elizabeth Garret Anderson hospital, but as she was now approaching sixty, it was ok for her to be staying in the women's ward!

About a week before she was due to have the procedure, dad's old neighbour telephoned me to say she had been having a clear out and had found a box of toys in a cupboard in the outside lobby of dad's old flat and did we want to have a look or should she throw them away. I thought we had better have a look, but it could wait a couple of weeks, until my sister had finished her stay in hospital.

That evening I telephoned my sister to tell her of the neighbour's call and she said, could we go the next day to see the toys! I met her in front of the flat the next morning and I had a funny feeling in my tummy as to what was about to occur. My sister said she had been asking mum what she should take to hospital with her this time, now the teddy bears were gone, as we hadn't seen them for fifty years and certainly hadn't come across them when we were clearing the flat.

The kind neighbour walked us to a side room where she had left the box and yes, inside were the two white teddy bears!! Needless to say, after giving the bears a wash, my sister took them to hospital with her.

How absolutely amazing that although mum is now operating from another dimension, she got those teddy bears to my sister, exactly when she needed them.

The Magic of Knowing

The magic of knowing
you still walk by my side,
fills my heart with a happiness
I don't wish to hide.

I thank you so much
for letting us see,
the world you now live in,
that's so close to me.

I know that one day,
we will walk there together.
Share a hug,
share a smile,
for we'll then share forever.

Composed by Angela

My writing became more spiritual after Jessica's passing and I found expressing my grief through the creation of a poem very therapeutic.

As soon as I am comfortable with the finished piece of poetry, I send it to all my friends. It's like releasing loving energy into the universe. I only ever write with loving intentions.

The poems seemed to be helpful to others who had lost a loved one and friends suggested I publish them.

I decided I would write an introduction to each of the poems I chose to publish and the idea for a little book began to take shape in my mind.

GONE IN AN INSTANT - SO WHAT HAPPENS NEXT?

So, how to publish my poems, where to start!

I knew two things. Firstly I wanted the cover of the book to be a picture of Jessica. Not a photograph, a picture, like it had been painted. My sister had taken a photograph of Jessica at a family gathering a couple of months before she died. We were spending the weekend in Witney, Oxfordshire a favourite destination for our whole family. In the photo, Jessica's face is a bit shiny, so my sister asked the photographic developers to take out the shine. The results were lovely and looked more like a painting.

This beautiful photograph was placed beside the coffin at Jessica's funeral. I had never seen this done before at any funeral I have ever attended and was anxious that some of the family or Jessica's friends may be upset by it. However, the sight of Jessica's lovely smile at such a difficult time gave us courage to sit through the service.

Secondly, I wanted to talk about Jessica in the book containing the poetry, but I hadn't imagined that the book would evolve as the story of her young life here on Earth and the astounding fact that since her death, she lets us know, frequently, that she is still close to us! Because Jessica makes such an effort to give us evidence that she survives, somewhere in another dimension, I felt I should share this knowledge to give comfort and hope to others. I know she would want me to do that.

Somehow, with Jessica's amazing contribution, the love and support from my friends and family and no doubt, the angels, I managed to finish Gone In An Instant – So What Happens Next?

In fact, the angels actually found a way to let me know that they approved of the little book. When I first did a word count of my work there were 1111 lines! This is a very special number for the angels and indicates the

Divine is crossing your path and you are experiencing a spiritual awakening in order to assist and inspire the human race. Wow! Or as Jessica would say, Holy Moses mummy!

I have found such joy in creating poetry and like to think that when someone reads one of my poems, they may experience laughter, tears, comfort, wonder or even inspiration to have a go at writing their own poetry.

A neighbour of mine, who became a close friend when we lived next door to each other, was inspired to write a poem. For over twenty years we enjoyed many walks in the forest as part of the Neighbourly Walkers, consuming mountains of cheese rolls and ginger cake at the green hut!

After reading Gone In An Instant. So What Happens Next? she was inspired to write something for me. One day as she was out walking her dog, she thought of an idea and when she got home she put pen to paper and wrote such a profound piece of poetry.

I think that the poem is beautiful, describing the emotions and intentions of the book's author (me!) perfectly. I asked her permission to use the poem in this book and she kindly agreed when I promised more glorious portions of ginger cake.

So much happiness evolves from the baking and eating of cake!

Angela

I have a friend called Angela
she lives not far away.
She wrote a book about love and hope
I read the other day.

The book was borne of tragedy
too hard to comprehend.
But through her grief and tears and pain
some hope she'd like to send.

To others who have felt the same
and some who may not yet know,
how easily our life can change
in one cruel fatal blow.

But with faith in God and strength of mind
a loving book of hope,
has risen from her loving heart
and shows that we might cope.

A reason to move forward
look ahead not to the past.
Look for signs in daily life,
little things that cross your path.

Have faith and know that loved ones past
can help us day by day,
to understand how in time we can
be reunited in some way.

So anyone who's in this place
of hopelessness and sorrow.
Take time to read this lovely book
and you will know tomorrow.

That there is hope and there is peace
there is a brighter place.
For our journey isn't over
when our body leaves this space.

We continue into heaven
where our loved ones were before
and our time on Earth has finished,
we're not needed anymore.

So Angela my "Angel"
I salute your heart and mind
and I know that in my future life,
your friendship I'll always find.

Composed by my very good friend and neighbour
Denise
August 2015

WHEN IS THE END NOT THE END?
WHEN IT'S THE BEGINNING!

When Jessica passed from this life to the next, she was living away from home in Selly Oak, Birmingham, where she was studying Ancient History at The University of Birmingham.

We didn't learn the devastating news of her death until late in the evening, so when I awoke that October morning, I was totally unaware of how my day would end. The moment I opened my sleepy eyes, I felt overwhelmingly happy! Every part of my body was energized with love and wellbeing.

As I drove to work at Fidgety Fingers that morning, I was singing all the songs from The Sound Of Music, one of Jessica's favourite films, which she had loved since she was a little girl. I was singing so loudly I had to close the car windows so as not to cause a disturbance! All through the day I was fit to burst with happiness and I kept asking myself, why am I soooo happy today?

I believe Jessica had already passed from this life and the love that was surrounding her at the beginning of her new life, was embracing me also!

How can anyone say for certain what is actually awaiting us at the End, until we arrive there ourselves? Of course, all of us are going to experience the death of the physical body, which is nature's course. However, what happens to us next is still a fascinating mystery.

Scientists all over the world are doing their very best to discover the invisible dimensions of energy that exist all around us and there is evidence of progress in their efforts.

As for my thoughts on the question that has been asked since the beginning of time "Is there life after death?" I can honestly say I believe there is! Now you have had the opportunity of wandering through my mind and digested the revelations of loving communications from another dimension, what are your thoughts.........................

I hope you have enjoyed the poetry and true stories you have read whilst following your pathway through my mind. Perhaps you will be inspired to write a poem or a book, but most especially, to investigate our great big never ending universe!

Wishing you amazing adventures
great and small!

Angela

Photograph on front cover: Taken in the Peak District by Angela.